WOMEN MYSTICS

of the

CONTEMPORARY ERA

Thierry Gosset

WOMEN MYSTICS
of the
CONTEMPORARY ERA

Nineteenth - twentieth centuries
An anthology

Translated from the French
by
Wendy Brennan

ST PAULS

WOMEN MYSTICS OF THE CONTEMPORARY ERA: An anthology
Originally published in French by La Table Ronde with the title
Femmes Mystiques: Epoque contemporaine

This translation © St Pauls. First published, 2003

North American edition published by Alba House, 2187 Victory Blvd,
Staten Island NY 10314-6603, USA http://www.albahouse.org
ISBN 0-8189-0943-9   Three Volume Set (ISBN 0-8189-0944-7)

UK-Ireland edition published by ST PAULS Publishing, 187 Battersea
Bridge Road, London SW11 3AS, UK http://www.stpauls.ie
ISBN 0-85439-658-6   Three Volume Set (ISBN 0-85439-662-4)

Australian edition published by ST PAULS PUBLICATIONS
Society of St Paul, 60-70 Broughton Road - PO Box 906
Strathfield, NSW 2135 AUSTRALIA   http://www.stpauls.com.au
ISBN 1-876295-51-1

National Library of Australia
Cataloguing-in-Publication Data:
Femmes mystiques: Epoque contemporaine English.
Women Mystics of the Contemporary Era: An anthology
1. Women mystics. 2. Mysticism - Catholic Church - History - 19th
century. 3. Mysticism - Catholic Church - History - 20th century.
4. Christian women saints. I. Gosset, Thierry. II. Brennan, Wendy
248.22082

Cover design by Ellie Exarchos
Printed and bound in Australia by McPherson's Printing Group

ST PAULS PUBLICATIONS is an activity of the Priests and Brothers of
the Society of St Paul who place at the centre of their lives the mission
of evangelisation with the means of social communication.

Contents

Introduction 7

Thérèse of Lisieux 11

Elizabeth of the Trinity 29

Edith Stein 47

Simon Weil 65

Marthe Robin 83

Introduction

I n contrast with preceding periods, the eighteenth and nineteenth centuries are poor in feminine spiritual literature. The controversy caused by the Enlightenment and Jansenism occupied the intellectual and religious scene of the time.

It was not until the second half of the nineteenth century before a new mystical flame rekindled and rose up again. New vocations blossomed against a background of positivism[1] and atheistic humanism.[2] Thérèse of the Child Jesus is the first great mystic to emerge in this period. 'My vocation is love!' she exclaimed (*Story of a Soul*). Love illumined the whole of her short life. She is the mystic of 'the little way'. With Thérèse, the spirit

of abandonment [3] which is characteristic of Carmel, took on a new meaning and returned to spirituality and Thérèse, despite the terrible darkness towards the end of her life, lived out this abandonment.

Elizabeth of the Trinity, unlike Thérèse, sought above all to disappear 'into the bosom of the Three'.

> Oh, why do you make me languish?
> I want so much to belong to you
> And to live with you in solitude
> Far from those I love on earth
>
> *(Complete Works)*

Edith Stein, a third great Carmelite of the contemporary period, was certainly the most original. A converted Jewish philosopher, she was attracted by the human qualities and the radical gift of self of Teresa of Avila (see *Women Mystics of the Modern Era*).

Two astonishing women conclude this anthology of contemporary women mystics – Simone Weil

and Marthe Robin. Simone Weil was a woman of energy and full of generosity. Marthe Robin, in contrast, was virtually immobile for fifty years of her life due to illness. However, both of these women were in their own way ahead of their time: Simone the mystical philosopher on her quest for the absolute; and Marthe the stigmatic of Château-neuf-de-Galaure, the mystic through her 'lay' prophetic intuitions.

Mystics have to find new ways of expressing themselves in each age. The great mystics of the past were creative. Nothing is more mobile than the Spirit 'who blows where He will'. 'He created all the old forms and he has to create new forms' (Edith Stein).

THIERRY GOSSET

Notes

[1] *Positivism* is a way of thinking which recognises only positive facts and observable phenomena. It rejects concerns about being and knowing and it rejects belief in the existence of a God who reveals Godself.

[2] *Humanism* is a thought system concerned with human matters (and not divine ones) or with the human race (and not the individual) or with humankind as intellectual beings.

[3] This spirit of *abandonment* is that of abandonment *to God* in which one renounces one's own will in favour of conforming with God's will.

Thérèse of Lisieux

1873 – 1897

'I am a very little soul who can
offer God only very little things.'

TO MOTHER MARIE DE GONZAGUE

Thérèse Martin, born on 2 January 1873 at
Alencon, was the youngest of Zélie and Louis
Martin's five daughters. Her life was marked by
four major periods. The first, which was pleasant
and happy ended when she was four in 1877 with
the death of her mother. The second which lasted
ten years was dominated by torments caused by
oversensitivity. The third began at Christmas 1886
when she was thirteen. She described this as
starting with 'the night of light' and as 'the most
beautiful of all, the one most filled with heavenly

graces.' The final period corresponded to the last spiritual night during which Thérèse was determined despite terminal illness, to continue to believe as she had done when she was younger and healthier.

From the turning point of her mother's death, Thérèse's life was a succession of joys and great trials that arose from her delicate health. When her sister Pauline (whom she regarded as her second mother) became a Carmelite nun in 1882 she became more grief stricken. At that time she was only nine but seemed aware of her vocation. In 1887, when she was fourteen, she showed an ardent desire to become a Carmelite; three of her sisters were already religious – two of them Carmelites – but Thérèse had to wait until 9 March 1888 to follow them. She took the habit in the following year January of 1889 and received the name, Thérèse 'of the Child Jesus'. In September 1890 she took her final vows and added 'and the Holy Face' to her religious name. She knew she

had become a Carmelite 'to save souls and above all to pray for priests'. In July 1894, after their father's death, her sister Pauline (Mother Agnes) asked Thérèse to write her memoirs. She finished these in January 1896 and they became known as manuscript A - *The Story of Soul*. She wrote two other manuscripts completed in September 1896 and June 1897. The last one was edited by Mother Agnes but it was very different from the original and caused much controversy seemingly because she cut out parts of it which she did not want to go beyond convent walls. From Easter 1896 (when a second sign of tuberculosis showed) until her death at the age of twenty four on the 30 September 1897, Thérèse experienced both the dark night and the 'light in the night'.

Thérèse's reading sources were varied: *The Imitation of Christ, the Conferences of Abbé Arminjon, Teresa of Avila, John of the Cross, St Francis de Sales.*

Thérèse was a soul of exceptional breadth, ingenious as well as courageous and revolu-

tionary. She felt she had the vocations of a warrior, a priest, an apostle, a doctor of the Church and a martyr because, in her intimate communion with Christ which had placed her at the heart of the Church, she felt keenly all the different needs to which these various vocations respond. We must not be mistaken about her 'little way' which is a way of confident abandonment to Love, and has nothing to do with mawkishness or sentimentality that a superficial reading of Thérèse can associate with her. Thérèse called her spiritual combat which began at Easter 1896 a 'trial of faith'. She had a deep compassion for lost souls – 'it is so easy to go astray in the flowery paths of the world!' – and it is this that makes Thérèse very much our contemporary and opens the way to the twenty-first century.

The following extracts are translated from *L'Histoire d'une áme* (Office central de Lisieux, 1923 and 1925) and from the *Pœsies* (Office central de Lisieux, 1913; Cerf/Desclé de Brouwer, 1995).

Chapter 9

I must accept myself just as I am, with my many imperfections; but I am going to look for a little way to get to heaven that is very direct, very short, a completely new little way.

Chapter 10

If the canvas an artist is painting on could think and speak, surely it would not complain if the artist constantly touched and retouched it with his brush, and it would not envy the lot of that tool because it would realise that it owes its beauty not to the brush but to the artist using it. The brush, for its part, could not take the credit for the masterpiece produced through it; it would know that artists are never deterred because they make light of difficulties, and sometimes they are happy to use the poorest and most imperfect tools.

My dear Mother, I am a little brush that Jesus has chosen to paint his likeness in the souls you have

entrusted to me. Although an artist may have several brushes, he must have at least one for each of two particular purposes: one, the more useful, to apply the main colours and to cover the canvas quickly in a short time; the other, a smaller brush, to paint in the detail. Mother, you are the precious brush that Jesus holds lovingly in his hand and uses when he wants to do some great work in the souls of your children and I am the little brush that he deigns to use afterward for detail...

It is not because God has kept me from mortal sin that I go to him with confidence and love. I feel that even if I had on my conscience all the sins that anyone could commit, I would lose none of my confidence, but I would go, my heart broken with sorrow, and throw myself into the arms of my Saviour. I know how he loves the prodigal child; I have heard his words to the holy Magdalene, to the adulterous woman and to the Samaritan woman. No, no one could make me afraid, for I know what I believe about his love and his mercy.

I know that all this multitude of offences would disappear in a flash like a drop of water thrown into a burning furnace.

Chapter 11

To be your spouse, O Jesus; to be a Carmelite; to be, through my union with you, the mother of souls; all that would not be enough for me. However, I feel I have other vocations: I feel the vocation to be a warrior, a priest, an apostle, a doctor, and a martyr… I want to accomplish all the most heroic deeds; I feel I have the courage to be a crusader and I want to die on the battlefield defending the Church.

The priestly vocation! With what love I would carry you in my hands when my voice brought you down from heaven! With what love I would give you to souls! But, alas, while I desire to be a priest, I admire and envy the humility of St Francis of Assisi, and I feel called to imitate him by refusing

the sublime dignity of the priesthood. How can I bring together these different callings?

I would like to enlighten souls as the prophets and doctors did. I would like to travel the world, my Beloved, to preach your name and plant your glorious cross on pagan soil! But one mission would not be enough for me: simultaneously, I would want to make the Gospel known in all parts of the world and to the most distant islands. I would like to be a missionary, not only for a few years, but to have been one since the creation of the world, and to continue to be one until the end of the ages.

Yet, above all, I would like martyrdom. Martyrdom! The dream of my youth, it has grown with me in my little cell in Carmel. But this is another folly, for I do not want one form of torture. To satisfy me, I would need them all.

Like you, my adorable Spouse, I would like to be scourged and crucified. I would like to be flayed

alive like St Bartholomew; plunged into boiling oil like St John; I desire, like St Ignatius of Antioch, to be ground by the teeth of wild beasts so as to become bread worthy of God. With St Agnes and St Cecilia, I would like to offer my neck to the sword; and like Joan of Arc at the burning stake, to whisper the name of Jesus!

Chapter 4

I have compassion for souls that get lost! It is so easy to go astray on the flowery paths of the world! Undoubtedly, for a soul that has advanced a little, the sweetness that the world offers is mixed with bitterness, and fleeting praises cannot fill the immense void of the desires. But, I repeat, if my heart had not been raised to God from its first awakening, if the world had smiled on me from my entrance into this life, what would have become of me?

Thérèse of Lisieux

Chapter 5

The cry of the dying Jesus, 'I thirst', kept re-echoing in my heart and kindled an unknown and very ardent flame. I wanted to quench my Beloved's thirst. I felt myself thirsting for souls and I wanted, no matter what the cost, to snatch sinners from eternal flames.

My good Master, to encourage my zeal, immediately showed me that he was pleased with my desires. I heard about a great criminal, called Pranzini, who was condemned to death for horrible murders, and whose impenitence put him in danger of eternal damnation. I wanted to prevent this final and irreversible misfortune and, to attain this, I used all the spiritual means imaginable. Knowing that I could do nothing myself, I offered up for his ransom the infinite merits of Our Lord and the treasures of the Church.

Must I say it? I felt certain in the depths of my heart that my prayer would be heard, but to give myself

courage to continue running to win over souls, I made this naïve prayer: 'My God, I am sure that you will pardon the unfortunate Pranzini; I would believe it even if he did not make his confession and gave no other sign of repentance because I have such confidence in your infinite mercy. But, because he is my first sinner, I am asking you only for a *sign*, for my own consolation.'

My prayer was answered to the letter! Although Papa did not let us read the newspapers, I did not think I was being disobedient by looking at the lines about Pranzini. The day after his execution, I quickly opened the newspaper, *La Croix*, and what did I see? My tears betrayed my emotion and I had to flee. Pranzini, without confession, without absolution, had climbed onto the scaffold and the executioners were dragging him towards the fatal platform when, moved by a sudden inspiration, he turned round, seized a crucifix that the priest was holding out to him and kissed the sacred wounds three times! ...

Thérèse of Lisieux

I know God had no need of anyone to fulfil his work of sanctification but, just as he allows a clever gardener to grow rare and delicate plants by giving him the necessary scientific knowledge to do this while he himself takes care of making them fruitful, in the same way, he wants to be helped in his divine cultivation of souls. What would happen if a clumsy horticulturalist did not graft his trees properly? If he did not know which tree was which and wanted to graft, for example, roses onto a peach tree?

STORY OF A SOUL

My Song for Today

(Melody: 'Dieu de paix et de l'amour')

My life is an instant, a passing hour,
   my life is a moment that escapes me
   and flees.
You know, O my God, that to love you on
   earth, I have nothing but today!

Oh! Jesus I love you and my hearts longs for
      you …
for just one day, be my gentle support;
come reign in my heart, give me your smile,
   just for today!

Lord, what does it matter if the future is dark!
To ask you for tomorrow, oh! no …
   I cannot do that …
Keep my heart pure, cover me with your shadow,
   just for today!

If I dream about tomorrow, I fear my fickleness,
I feel in my heart, sad and weary;
but, my God, I do desire trials and suffering,
   just for today!

Thérèse of Lisieux

On this earth,
    there is a wonderful tree:
it's root, O mystery!
is found in heaven.
Nothing, living in its shade,
is ever harmed.
There, without fear of the storm,
we can rest.
From this extraordinary tree,
called *Love*,
comes its delicious fruit
called *abandonment*.

This fruit, already in this life,
brings me happiness;
its divine fragrance
brings joy to my soul.
This fruit, when I touch it,
is like a treasure to me;
when I put it in my mouth,

it is even sweeter to my taste.
It gives me, in this world,
an ocean of peace,
and in this profound peace,
I remain forever.

Only *abandonment* brings me
into your arms, O Jesus!
It nourishes me
with the bread of your elect.
I abandon myself to you,
O my divine Spouse!
I seek only
your very gentle gaze.
I want to keep on smiling,
while I sleep on your Heart …
And there, I want to say again
that I love you, Lord!

Thérèse of Lisieux

To my Guardian Angel

(Melody: '*Par les chants les plus magnifiques*')

Glorious guardian of my soul,
you who shine in the beautiful heavens
like a gentle and pure flame
near the throne of the Eternal One.
You come down on this earth for me
and enlighten me with your splendour.
Beautiful angel, you are my brother,
my friend, my consoler!

Knowing my great weakness, 0
you lead my by the hand;
and I see you gently
remove the stone from my path.
Your gentle voice keeps on telling me
to keep my eyes fixed on heaven;
the more humble and little you see me,
the more radiant is your face.

You who pass through space
more swiftly than light,
come very often and take my place

beside those who are dear to me.
Dry their tears with your wings.
Sing of God's goodness!
Sing that suffering has its delights,
and very softly whisper my name.

During my short life, I want
to save my brothers who are sinners.
O beautiful Angel from the homeland,
give me your holy ardour.
I have nothing but my sacrifices
and my simple poverty:
unite them with your pure delights
and offer them to the Trinity.

The kingdom and glory are yours,
the riches of the King of kings.
The bread from the sacred ciborium is mine,
the treasure of the Cross is mine.
With the Cross, with the Host,
with your heavenly help,
I wait in peace, from the other life,
the happiness that lasts forever!

POEMS

Elizabeth of the Trinity

1880 – 1906

'Calm my soul, make in it your heaven,
your beloved dwelling and your resting place.'

21 NOVEMBER 1904

Elizabeth Catez was born on 18 July 1880 near Bourges and like Therese of Lisieux, experienced illness at a very early age. Her sister Marguerite was born when she was three years old. Their father died suddenly in 1887 and this no doubt contributed to Elizabeth's growing awareness of her contemplative vocation. She was exuberant and passionate and an extremely gifted pianist, winning first prize at the Conservatorium at the age of thirteen.

A decisive meeting took place in 1900 with Père Vallée, a Dominican, who was together with Mother Marie of Jesus (the Prioress of Dijon Carmel) one of the first people to realise Elizabeth's spiritual genius. According to Didier Decoin in his book *Elizabeth Catez*, until that meeting Elizabeth 'had been like a very finely crafted violin enclosed in its case ... a note was struck.'

The eleven year old Elizabeth entered the Dijon Carmel on 2 August 1901 and took the name, Elizabeth 'of the Trinity'. From the age of fifteen Elizabeth entered a period of darkness and pain, weakened by Addison's disease. She took the name, *Laudem Gloriae* 'praise of glory' (borrowed from St Paul, cf. Eph 1:6). A praise of glory is 'the soul that lives in God'. This was her third and last name. Elizabeth died on 9 November 1906 aged sixteen after a long Calvary.

Elizabeth was a great contemplative. In her intimate talk with God and in her silence and adoration, she typifies the mystic caught up with the indwelling of the three divine persons in the soul. Writers such as Ruysbroeck, St Teresa of Avila and St John of the Cross, fully validate her spiritual journey. Her work consists of numerous spiritual treatises and letters.

'I am going to Light, to Love, to Life' were her last murmured words.

The following extracts are translated from *Souvenirs* (Carmel of Dijon, 1911).

A Praise of Glory

I have found my vocation; since I will be a praise of glory for all eternity, I want to be *a praise of glory* already here below!...

A praise of glory is a soul that lives in God, who loves him with a pure and disinterested love without thinking about herself in the sweetness of his love. It is a soul who loves him more than all his gifts and, even if that soul had received nothing from him, she desires the good of the Object she loves. Now, how can we truly desire and will God's goodness if not by doing it, since that will orders all things to his greater glory? Therefore, this soul must give herself up completely, passionately, so that it becomes impossible for her to will anything other than what God wills.

A praise of glory is a silent soul that is like a lyre waiting for the mysterious touch of the Holy Spirit to bring forth from it divine harmonies. The soul knows that suffering is a chord that produces even more beautiful sounds, and she loves to see herself used as his instrument to move more deeply the heart of her God.

A praise of glory is a soul that contemplates God in faith and simplicity. She is a reflection of all that He is; she is like an abyss in which He can flow and open His heart. She is also a crystal through which He can shine and contemplate his perfections and his own splendour. A soul that allows the divine Being to fulfil in her his need to communicate all that He is and all that He possesses is, in truth, the praise of glory of all his gifts.

Finally, a praise of glory is a being who is always giving thanks; whose actions, movements, thoughts and aspirations, while rooting her ever more deeply in love, are like an echo of the eternal

Elizabeth of the Trinity

Sanctus. In heavenly glory, the blessed rest neither day nor night, saying: '*Holy, Holy, Holy, all-mighty Lord ...*' and, prostrating, they adore the One who lives forever. In the heaven of her soul, the praise of glory begins already the office that will be hers for all eternity; her canticle is uninterrupted and she lives under the influence of the Holy Spirit. She may not always be aware of this, because human frailty does not allow her to keep her attention constantly fixed on God. She always sings, she always adores. She is, so to speak, wholly given to praise and love, passionate about the glory of her God.

In the heaven of our soul, let us be praises of the glory of the Holy Trinity. One day the veil will fall and we will be led through the divine portals; there, we will sing in the bosom of infinite Love, and God will give us the new name promised to those who are victorious. What will it be? - *Laudem Gloriae.*

A Praise of Glory. Day 1

'*Nescivi!* I no longer knew anything.' This is what the Spouse in the Canticles sings after she was led into the inner cellar (cf. Song 6:2). I think this must also be *a praise of glory's refrain* on this first day of retreat, when the Master leads her down into the abyss to teach her how to fulfil the office that will be hers for all eternity and which she must fulfil already in time, that is, the beginning of eternity that is always ongoing.

Nescivi! I no longer know anything; I no longer want anything, except to know Him and to share his sufferings and death (cf. Phil 3:10). Those whom God has foreknown, He has predestined to be conformed in the likeness of his Son (cf. Rom 8:29), the One crucified for love. When I shall become like this divine Model, I in Him and He in me, I shall fulfil my eternal vocation, the one which

God has chosen for me in Him *in principio* and which I shall carry out *in aeternum* when, plunged into the bosom of the Trinity, I will be the endless praise of his glory, *in laudem gloriae ejus* (cf. Eph 1:12).

'No-one has seen the Father, except the Son and those to whom it pleases the Son to reveal him' (cf. Jn 1:18). We can also add that no-one has ever penetrated the depths of the mystery of Christ, except the Virgin. St Paul often speaks of the understanding he received (cf. Eph 3:3), and yet, like all the saints, he was in darkness in comparison with the lights the Virgin received. The secret that she kept and pondered in her heart is beyond words: no tongue has been able to reveal it, no pen able to describe it.

This Mother of grace is going to form my soul so that her little child might be a living image, resembling her first-born (cf. Col 1:15), the Son of the Eternal, who was so perfectly: a praise of the glory of his Father.

'In God my soul is silent; I await my deliverance from Him. Yes, He is the Rock where I find my refuge, my stronghold, and I shall not be moved' (Ps 61/62 : 2-3/1-2).

This is the mystery my lyre plays every day. Just as my divine Master said to Zacchaeus: 'Make haste and come down, for I must stay at your house'(cf. Lk 19:5). 'Make haste and come down', but *where*? - To the deepest depths of my being, after I have been detached, separated and stripped of self; in a word, made selfless.

'I must stay at your house.' This is how my Master expresses his desire to me, my Master who wants to dwell in me with the Father and his Spirit of Love so that I might have *fellowship* with them (cf. 1 Jn 1:3). 'You are no longer visitors or strangers, but you already are part of God's household', said St Paul (cf. Eph 2:19).

This is how I understand the words, 'of God's household': it is living in the depths of the tranquil Trinity, in my interior abyss, in that impregnable fortress of holy recollection, of which St John of the Cross speaks.

'My soul longs and faints on entering the courts of the Lord' (cf. Ps 83/84 : 3/2).

This must be the disposition of my whole soul when I enter the interior *courts* to contemplate God and to make contact with him there. My soul faints away, in a divine swoon, before that all powerful love, that infinite majesty that dwells within. It is not that life leaves the soul; but rather it is she who despises this natural life and withdraws from it, for she feels she is unworthy of his essence that is so rich, she will die from it and slip away into her God.

Oh! How beautiful is this creature that is stripped and freed of self! She is in a state of 'readiness for the ascents of her heart, to pass through the valley of tears (that is, from all that is less than God), to

the place that is her goal' (cf. Ps 83/84 : 7/6), that spacious place, which is the unfathomable Trinity: *Immensus Pater, immensus Filius, immensus Spiritus Sanctus* (St Athanasius).

She goes up, she rises above her senses, above nature; she leaves herself behind, going beyond all joy and sorrow, and passes through the clouds to rest only when she penetrates *the depths* of the One she loves and who will give her *the peace of the abyss.* And all that, without having to leave the holy fortress because the divine Master has said to her: 'Make haste and come down.'

Without having to leave that place, she will live in the unchanging Trinity in *an eternal present*, adoring the Trinity forever for itself alone, and becoming through an ever simpler and more unifying gaze, 'the splendour of its glory' (cf. Heb 1:3), in other words: the unending *praise of glory* of the adorable perfections of the Trinity.

Prayer of Sr Elizabeth of the Trinity

O my God, Trinity whom I adore, help me to forget myself completely so that I might be at home with you, as still and as peaceful as if my soul were already in eternity. Let nothing disturb my peace nor make me leave you, my Changeless One, but may each minute carry me ever deeper into the depths of your Mystery. Calm my soul; make it your heaven, your beloved dwelling and resting place. May I never leave you there alone but be wholly present with you, with enkindled faith, in complete adoration and totally surrendered to your creative action.

O my Christ, crucified for love, I want to be the bride of your heart; I want to cover you with glory, I want to love you … until I die of it. But I know my powerlessness, and I am asking you to clothe me with Yourself, to identify my soul with all the movements of your soul, to overwhelm me, to inundate me, to substitute yourself for me, so that my life might be but a radiance of Your life. Come into me as Restorer and Saviour.

O eternal Word, Word of my God, I want to spend my life listening to you, I want to become wholly teachable so that I might learn all from you. Then, through all nights, all voids and all powerlessness, I want to keep my gaze fixed always on you and live in your great light. O my beloved Star, so fascinate me that I am unable to leave your radiance.

O consuming Fire, Spirit of Love, overshadow me so that my soul might become as it were an incarnation of the Word, that I might be another humanity for him in which he can renew all his

mystery. And you, Father, bend lovingly over your poor little creature, seeing in her only the Beloved in whom you take all your delight.

O my 'Three', my all, my happiness, infinite Solitude, Immensity in which I lose myself, I surrender myself to you as your prey. Hide yourself within me so that I might hide myself within you, while I am waiting to go and contemplate in your light the abyss of your greatness.

21 NOVEMBER 1904

A Carmelite is a soul who has contemplated the divine Crucified One. She has seen him offering himself as a victim to the Father and, pondering on this great vision of Christ's love, she has understood his loving passion and wanted to give herself to him. On Mount Carmel, in silence and solitude, in constant prayer, she lives as if she were in heaven, for God alone! She has a foretaste of the happiness and fulfilment that will one day be hers in glory. He does not leave her; He dwells in her soul and, more than that, the two become one and she thirsts for silence to keep on listening, to enter ever more deeply into his Infinite Being. She becomes one with the One she loves and finds him everywhere. Is this not heaven on earth? You carry this heaven within you, for Jesus knows the Carmelite *within*, that is, by her soul. Never leave him, do everything under his divine gaze, and live joyously in his peace and his love.

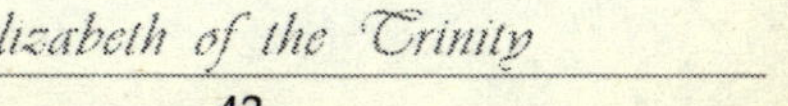

Elizabeth of the Trinity

Heaven in the Soul

O Lord, I want to disappear in you
like a drop of water in an immense sea;
deign to destroy in me what is not divine,
so that my soul, being free, rushes into your Being.

I have to enter that *immense space*,
that fathomless abyss and that profound mystery
so as to love you, Jesus, as you are loved in heaven,
without any external thing able to distract me.

I want to live in your 'foyer of love',
in the ray of lights shining forth from your Face;
and live for you alone as in the divine dwelling
   place,
in that sweet peace that is beyond compare.

There, this transformation will take place,
there I will become like another you;
but I will only attain that state
by losing everything here below for you, Supreme
   Beauty.

When we truly love we no longer live in ourselves,
for we feel the need to forget ourselves constantly;
the heart only finds rest and refreshment
when it has found the object of its love.

That is why, Jesus, in my love for you,
I desire naught but your holy presence;
at every moment of the day, I want to forget myself
and, in your sight alone, offer myself up in silence.

In the profound peace of your eternal Being,
deign to hide me away in you so that, while still in
   this life,
I can live as if I were in heaven,
in your love and infinite peace.

I do not have to look for you outside
to become one with you;
I have only to hide myself within my heart
to lose myself forever in your divine Essence.

POEMS. AUGUST 1906

Elizabeth of the Trinity

A Meeting Place for Laudem Gloriae and her Sister

I am going to arrange an intimate meeting place
    for us,
a secret, divine and mysterious meeting place …
My sister, let us hide in the depths of *the double
      abyss*,
where we can wait for the sweet peace of heaven.

Let us know how to take the last place,
so as to be like Jesus our Spouse;
then the light from his Face will shine on us,
for he is drawn towards the lowly and gentle!

For, if we are to live constantly in his presence,
we have to be annihilated; that is the condition.
Oh! Let abasement be our home,
our royal palace, our dwelling place.

POEMS. SEPTEMBER 1906

Edith Stein

1891 – 1942

'The soul's silence is of greater
value than a thousand words.'

THE SCIENCE OF THE CROSS

Edith was born into an established Jewish family in Breslau (Silesia). Her father died when she was very young and her mother had to take charge of running her deceased husband's timber business and the education of her eleven children. In 1911, Edith went to Breslau University where she studied mainly psychology, but she left the following year. She became an admirer of Edmund Husserl, the founder of phenomenology[4] and decided to continue her education at Göttingen. He had a decisive influence on her thinking and her life.

A second major event followed in 1921. While staying with friends in Bergzabern, she discovered a copy of *The Life of Teresa of Avila*. Her reading of this book did more than edify her: it directed her steps firmly towards the Christian faith. Edith was baptised in Bergzabern, on 1 January 1922. Her conversion seemed to be not so much a denial of her Jewish religion, but rather an affirmation of her identification with the Jewish people 'at the beginning of her life as a Christian' (Marguerite Léna).

From 1922 to 1932, Edith taught German at the Dominican college of St Magdalene in Speyer. She translated and made a commentary on St Thomas Aquinas' *De Veritas* which reoriented her thinking and spirituality towards exemplarism[5] (which had been so clearly set forth by Hadewijch of Antwerp).

On 14 October 1933 at the age of forty-two, Edith entered the Cologne Carmel where she became Sister Teresa Benedicta of the Cross. Her choice of title 'of the Cross' has a twofold explanation: its

reference to Christ and its reference to the tragic circumstances into which the Jewish people were thrown. A major work, *Finite Being and Eternal Being*, was published only after the war because of the Nazis' anti-Semitic laws.

From 1938 to 1942, Edith and her sister Rosa, who had also converted to Catholicism, sought refuge at the Carmelite Monastery in Echt (Holland). There, she wrote her outstanding, although unfinished, mystical work, *The Science of the Cross*. On 2 August 1942, the Gestapo arrested the two Carmelite sisters. They were taken to Auschwitz and were killed a week later – 9 August 1942.

Edith Stein was a great intellectual and mystical figure who confirms and highlights the vocation of women and their role in the interior renaissance of the Church and the world. She was proclaimed Blessed in 1987 and was canonised on Sunday, 11 October 1998, in Rome by Pope John-Paul II.

The following English translation of extracts from the works of Edith Stein is based on French translations of *La Science de la Croix* by Étienne de St Marie (Nauwelaerts, 1957), *La Puissance de la Croix* by Thomas Soriano (Nouvelle Cité, 1989), and *La Prière de l'Église* by L. and E. Zwianer (l'Orante, 1955).

Notes

[4] *Phenomenology* is the study of phenomena or objects which we can sense.

[5] *Exemplarism* refers to an understanding of finite things as copies or examples of divine ideas e.g. a real tree is an example of the divine idea of a tree.

The Soul in the Realm of the Spirit and Spirits

It is up to the soul to decide for herself. The great mystery concerning the freedom of the individual is that God himself stops before her. He wants to have dominion over created spirits who only freely give him their love. He knows the thoughts of the heart, he penetrates the depths and abysses of the soul that it would be unable to reach if God did not enlighten it in the appropriate manner. However, He does not want to take possession of the soul without the soul's consent, but He does everything so that the soul might freely surrender herself to his will and He might lead her to this blessed union. This is the Good News that John of the Cross wants to announce, that all his writings tend to make known.

THE SCIENCE OF THE CROSS

Edith Stein

Just as the torrent that bursts its bank submerges everything beneath its waters, fills all the deep places and drowns out every other noise with the roar of its waves, so the soul, in the same way, is empowered by 'this torrent that is the Spirit of God. He takes hold of her with such power that she feels as if all the rivers of the world were flooding in on her.' Yet, the vehemence of this flood does not cause her any pain, for they are rivers of peace, and their onslaught 'fills her completely with peace and glory'. The water fills the depths of her lowliness and the void of her desires, and in the whirlpool of the current, she hears 'a spiritual voice that … is louder than every other voice and is heard over all the noises of the world…'

It is a great thundering interior voice that fills the soul with strength and power, just as it did when it accompanied the descent of the Holy Spirit on the Apostles. This mighty wind that the inhabitants of Jerusalem heard was only a sign of

what the Apostles perceived interiorly. Despite its formidable power, this spiritual voice is gentle to the ear. St John perceived it as 'the roaring of mighty waters and the rolling sounds of thunder', and, at the same time, as 'a concert of harpists playing their harps' (Rev 14:2).[6]

It is like a gentle breeze that softly whistles and caresses the face, that instils into the soul the virtues and charms of the Beloved. 'It is a very lofty and very gentle knowledge of God and his perfections that comes to the understanding as a result of the touch that these virtues of God have had on the substance of the soul …'

'Just as we feel the breeze through our sense of touch and its sound through our hearing, in the same way we perceive and enjoy the touch of the perfections of the Beloved through the senses of the soul, that is to say, in its substance (by means of the will), and we acquire knowledge through the hearing of the soul by means of the intellect'. This communication is above all extremely

'delicious and delectable … As the soft whistle of the breeze is easily picked up by the hearing organ, this sweet and subtle knowledge penetrates with wonderful gentleness the innermost depths of the soul's substance. This last joy surpasses all others … because God gives the soul substantial knowledge free from all forms and images'. This divine *breeze* that enters the soul through its hearing is not only substantial knowledge, it is also a manifestation of divine truths to the intellect or a revelation of God's mysteries. Whenever Scripture speaks about a certain communication God has made … by means of the hearing, we can usually say that it is a revelation of these naked truths to the intellect. These are purely spiritual revelations or visions which are given only to the soul without assistance or help from the senses. For this reason, the knowledge that God communicates through the hearing … is very lofty and very certain. It is thought that this was how our holy Father Elijah saw God 'in a gentle breeze' (1 Kings 19:12) and how St Paul 'heard ineffable

words that no human being can reveal' (2 Cor 12:4). In fact, 'to hear with the hearing of the soul is like seeing with the help of the intellect'. Still, this is not the clear and perfect vision of God, as enjoyed in Glory, for it still remains 'a ray of darkness'.[7]

Because the soul receives this dark and impenetrable knowledge and tastes a comforting repose when she sleeps on the bosom of the Beloved, she likens it to the tranquil night. It is, however, a night already illumined by the light of the dawn, because it is a tranquillity and quietude in divine light and a new knowledge of God … when the light of dawn breaks forth, it is neither night-time nor daytime; it is rather … a twilight.[8]

In the tranquillity and silence of that light-studded night, 'the soul sees at last the properties and wonderful gifts of infinite Wisdom that shine forth in all the different creatures and works of God. All in general, as well as each in particular, manifest their dependence on God. Each in its own way sings what God is in it and the soul seems to hear

a sublime harmony that surpasses all the concerts and melodies here below'.[9] But the music is silent, for this quiet and tranquil knowledge is heard without any vocal sound.

In the Power of the Cross

At the time of my conversion, just before it happened, and even for a long time afterwards, I thought that to lead a religious life meant one had to renounce all worldly things, and think only about divine things. But, gradually, I came to understand that in this world something quite different is asked of us and that even in the most contemplative way of life we must not break our link with the world. I had even thought that the more we are 'drawn' into God, the more we must, in a sense, 'go out from self', that is, offer oneself for the world, so as to bring the divine life to it...

Because our natural understanding is unable to perceive the divine light, we must, through contemplation, be led towards darkness.

The work of Redemption is accomplished in secret and in silence. In the silent dialogue between the heart and God, the living stones with which the Kingdom of God is built are prepared and the chosen instruments needed for its construction are forged. The mystical stream, which flows through the centuries, is not a meandering side-stream that has separated from the prayer life of the Church; it is her very life-blood. If it breaks with traditional forms, it does so because the Spirit is living in it, a Spirit that blows where It wills. He created all the old forms and He has to create new ones. Without Him there would be neither liturgy nor Church. Was not the soul of the royal psalmist a harp whose strings sang when touched by the gentle breeze of the Holy Spirit? Did not the hymn of the *Magnificat* burst forth from the Virgin's joy-filled heart? And, in the same way, the prophetic chant of the *Benedictus* opened the dumb lips of the old priest Zechariah when the angel's secret

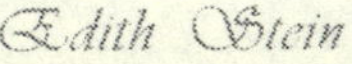

announcement was fulfilled. For what bursts forth from a heart filled with the Holy Spirit seeks expression in canticles and hymns and is passed on by word of mouth, and it is the work of the Divine Office to make it reverberate through the ages.

This mystical stream forms a symphony of praise to the Holy Trinity: to the Creator, the Redeemer and the Consoler. We cannot therefore put, on one side, prayer that is interior and free from all traditional form - 'subjective piety'; and, on the other side, the liturgy, which is 'objective prayer'. Every authentic prayer is a prayer of the Church: each sincere prayer brings about something in the Church, and it is the Church herself that prays, for the Holy Spirit that lives in her, lives also in each soul and 'prays for us with ineffable sighs'. This is real prayer for, unless a person is in the Holy Spirit, he or she cannot say: 'Lord Jesus'. What would the prayer of the Church be, if it were not the gift of those who love the God who is Love, with great love? The total gift of our heart to God and the gift He makes us in return -

complete and eternal union with Him - is the highest state we can attain, the highest degree of prayer. Souls that have attained it are truly the heart of the Church: the sacerdotal love of Jesus lives in them. With Christ, hidden in God, they can radiate to other hearts only the divine love they possess. In this way, they contribute to the perfection of all in union with God which, in the past as in the present, is Jesus' only desire.

This was how Marie-Antoinette de Geuser understood her vocation. She had to fulfil the Christian's highest duty in this world; and her way is certainly the most significant example for those today who feel urged to take on spiritually the responsibility of the Church and are unable to answer this call in the hidden life of a cloister. The soul that has reached the highest degree of mystical prayer in the tranquil activity of the divine life thinks only of giving herself to the apostolate to which God is calling her. 'It is tranquillity in order and, at the same time, activity freed from all fetters. The

soul campaigns for peace because she works in accordance with the eternal decrees. She knows that God's will is fulfilled perfectly for his greater glory, for if human will limits the all-powerful divine will, that all-powerful will still triumphs and does magnificent work with the materials left to it. This victory of God's power over human beings whom He leaves free to act nevertheless is one of the most adorable features of the divine plan.'

When Marie-Antoinette de Geuser wrote this letter, she was on the threshold of eternity and only a transparent veil still separated her from that ultimate perfection that we call the life of glory.

Everything is one for the blessed spirits who have reached the profound unity of the divine life: repose and action to contemplate and to work; to be silent and to speak; to listen and to pour out one's heart; to receive in oneself, in love, the divine gift and to return love with thanksgiving and praise.

As long as we are on the way, no matter how distant the goal seems, we live under the law of this earthly life and yet we are assured that, in the Mystical Body, through the mutual advancement of all its members, this divine life in all its fullness will become a reality for us.

During the hours of the Divine Office, we must listen in silence and let the divine word blossom in us until it prompts us to praise God during prayer and work.

We also need the traditional forms and we must take part in public worship, as the Church ordains, so that our interior life grows, stays on the right path and finds a way to express itself. There must be sanctuaries on earth where we can celebrate the solemn praise of God with all the perfection with which we are capable. From there, *in the name of* all the Church, the soul can ascend to heaven, influence all her members, enkindle their interior lives and spur them on in their efforts for others. But for this

Edith Stein

hymn of praise to arise from within, there still has to be these places of prayer reserved for deepening the spiritual life. Otherwise, this praise would degenerate into a mumbling with the lips devoid of all life. It is thanks to these places for the interior life that such danger is avoided: souls can meditate there before God in silence and solitude and be singers of this life-giving love in the heart of the Church.

Christ introduced us to this spiritual life through which we join with the choirs of heavenly spirits who sing the eternal *Sanctus*. His blood is like a veil through which we enter the Holy of Holies of the divine life. In baptism, and in the sacrament of penance, this blood cleanses us of our sins and opens our eyes to eternal light; our ears to the divine word; and our lips to praise, to penitential prayer, to prayer of petition, to thanksgiving. All of these, under different forms, constitute one single act of adoration, that is to say, the homage of the creature to the all-powerful and infinitely good God. In the

sacrament of confirmation, this blood marks and strengthens the soldier of Christ to profess his or her faith loyally. But in this sacrament, more than in all the others, Christ is present and we become members of his Body. While we are taking part in the Holy Sacrifice, in Holy Communion, we are being fed with the Body and Blood of Jesus, and we become ourselves his Body and Blood. It is only insofar as we are members of his Body that his Spirit can give us life and reign in us, '... it is the Spirit that gives life, for it is the Spirit that gives life to the members. He gives life only to those whom the Body, in which the Spirit acts, has already given life. The Christian's only fear is being separated from the Body of Christ. For, separated from the Body of Christ, he or she is no longer his member and will no longer receive life from the Spirit.' We become members of Christ's Body 'not only through love but in all truth through union with his flesh, a union that is brought about through the food He gives us to show us he thirsts for our love. This is why He came down among us and made his Body

like ours, so that we might be one as the body is one with the head.'

Members of his Body, animated by his Spirit, we offer ourselves as victim 'through Him, with Him and in Him', and we join in the eternal hymn of thanksgiving.

This is why the Church has us say, after Holy Communion:

> Filled with these wondrous gifts,
> we ask you, Lord, to grant
> that we might receive from them all the graces
> of salvation
> and never cease to sing your praise.

THE PRAYER OF THE CHURCH

Notes

[6] *Spiritual Canticle*, str. 14 (13), v. 4.
[7] Denys, the Areopagite, *De Mystica Theologica*, ch. 1.
[8] *Spiritual Canticle*, str. 15 (14), v. 1.
[9] *Spiritual Canticle*, str. 15 (14), v. 1.

Simone Weil

1909 - 1943

'Absolute and pure attention is prayer.'

GRAVITY AND GRACE

Simone was born in Paris on 3 Feb 1909 into a close and comfortably well off Jewish family. She had a happy childhood but World War 1 made her acutely sensitive to the miseries of humankind. She was a gifted child and brilliant pupil. Her contact with Alain, her professor at Henry IV College, from 1925 to 1928 filled her with an enthusiasm for ideas and equipped her with mental discipline.

In 1931, she began teaching at Le Puy, Roanne, Bourges but took leave to become a factory worker

from December 1934 to August 1935. Her time here was a crucial one where she experienced the inhumane conditions of the working class, first hand. She involved herself in political and trade union activities, helping with the unemployed, writing articles (in *La Critique sociale* and *La Revolution proletarienne)* and eventually moving on and taking part in the Spanish Civil War linking herself with the anarchists but maintaining an agnostic outlook.

In 1938, during Holy Week she went to Solesmes where she was swept away by the beauty of the Gregorian chant. It was here that she had an epiphanous experience after reading George Herbert's poem 'Love'. She said she experienced 'Christ taking possession of her'.

In June 1941 due to anti-Semitic laws she went to work in Provence as an agricultural labourer where she met Father J M Perrin and stayed as a guest with Gustave Thibon. This resulted in one of her most beautiful collections of writing, *Waiting*

for God, in which she writes about her intellectual problems preventing her from entering the Church.

In November 1942, Simone went to London to work for the Free French movement, but had only a few months left to live. On 15 April 1943, she was admitted to hospital with tuberculosis and it is possible she may have received baptism from a friend. However, on 24 August that year she died in the Ashford sanatorium, aged thirty-four.

Simone Weil struggled for social justice and equality, freedom of action and opinion, social activism and the promotion of peace, care for one's neighbour and universal faith.

> The following extracts are translated from *Attente de Dieu (Livre de vie, 1977)*, from *La Pesanteur et la Grâce (Plon, 1988)*, and from *Écrits de Londres (Gallimard, 1957)*.

I will finish by saying what concerns me. The kind of inhibition that keeps me outside the Church is due either to the state of imperfection in which I find myself or to its going against my vocation and God's will. In the first case, I am unable to get rid of this inhibition directly but only indirectly by becoming less imperfect, if grace helps me to do it. For this to come about, on the one hand, I have to try to avoid faults in the domain of natural things and, on the other, I have to put even more attention and love into thinking about God. If it is God's will for me to enter the Church, He will compel me to do his will when I will be worthy for him to ask me to do it.

In the second case, if it is not his will that I enter it, how could I enter it? I know that you have often told me that baptism is the common way to salvation - at least in Christian countries - and that there is absolutely no reason why I should

have a special way. That is clear. Yet, nevertheless, in case I was not meant to go that way, what would I do? If it were conceivable that I could be damned by obeying God and saved by disobeying him, I would still choose obedience.

I think it is not God's will for me to enter the Church now. For, as I have already told you, and it still holds true, I feel the inhibition that holds me back as strongly during moments of attention, love and prayer as at other times. And yet I felt a very great joy when I heard you say that my thoughts, as I had explained them to you, are not incompatible with belonging to the Church and that, consequently, I am not an outsider in spirit.

I cannot stop myself from wondering in these days, when such a large section of the human race is sunk in materialism, if God does not will that there might be some men and women who might give themselves to him and to Christ and who still, nevertheless, remain outside the Church.

Simone Weil

In any case, when I think about the formal act of entering the Church in practical terms, and as something that might be close, no thought gives me greater pain than that of separating myself from the vast and unfortunate mass of unbelievers. I have a basic need, and I think I can say a vocation, to go among men and women in different human environments, to mix with them, to adopt their views and opinions insofar as I am able and my conscience does not prevent me. I become one of them so that they can be themselves with me and lay aside their masks. I want to know them so I can love them just as they are. For if I do not love them as they are, I do not love them, and my love is not real. I am not talking about helping them for, unfortunately, up until now, I have been unable to do that. I think that in any case I would never enter a religious order because the habit would separate me from ordinary men and women. This separation is not a serious matter for some human beings because they are already separated from ordinary people by the natural purity of their soul.

But as for me, on the contrary, I think I have told you I have within me the seeds of all, or almost all, crimes. I became aware of this during a journey, in circumstances I told you about. The crimes horrified, but did not surprise, me; it is even because I felt it was possible for me to commit them that they filled me with horror. This natural disposition is dangerous and very distressing, but as with all natural dispositions they can be used for good if one knows how to put them to good use with the help of grace. There is a vocation to remain in some way anonymous, to be always ready to be mixed in the dough of common humanity. Now, today, in people's minds, there is a greater barrier, a more noticeable separation between a practising Catholic and an unbeliever than between religious and lay people.

I know Christ said: 'Whoever disowns me, I will disown before my Father'. But disowning Christ does not perhaps mean the same thing for everyone who does not belong to the Church. For

Simone Weil

some, it may mean only not living according to Christ's teachings, not radiating his spirit, not honouring his name when the opportunity comes along, not being ready to die faithful to him.

I owe you the truth at the risk of offending you and although it is extremely painful for me to offend you. I love God, Christ and the Catholic faith as far as it is possible for a miserably inadequate creature to love them. I love the saints through their writings and the accounts of their lives - apart from some whom it is impossible for me to love fully or to consider as saints. I love the six or seven truly spiritual Catholics whom I have chanced to meet during my life. I love the Catholic liturgy, hymns, architecture, rites and ceremonies. But I do not have any love for the Church properly so called, apart from its connection with these things that I love. I can sympathise with those who do have this love but I do not feel it. I know that all the saints experienced it. But then nearly all of them were born and brought up in the Church. Be that as it may, we

cannot will ourselves to love. All that I can say is that, if this love is a condition of spiritual progress of which I am unaware, or if it is part of my vocation, I desire that one day He might grant it to me.

Perhaps some of the thoughts I have just written down for you are misleading and bad. But, in a way, that matters little to me; I do not want to keep on going through it any more; for, after all these reflections, I have reached a conclusion which is the pure and simple decision not to give any more thought to my eventual entry into the Church.

It is quite possible that after I have stopped thinking about it for weeks, months or years, one day I will be suddenly impelled to ask for baptism immediately, and I will run and ask for it. For grace works in our hearts in a hidden and silent way.

It is also possible that my life will end without my ever having experienced this impulsion. But one thing is absolutely certain: if a day should come that I love God enough to merit the grace of baptism,

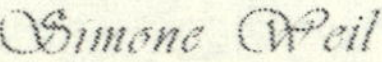

I will receive that grace on that same day, without fail, under whatever form God wills, whether it is by baptism properly so called, or by some other manner. Then why should I be concerned? It is not my business to think about me. My business is to think about God. It is God's business to think about me.

WAITING FOR GOD

Decreation

Why is it that when one human being shows a greater or lesser need for another he or she withdraws? Gravity...

We possess only what we renounce. What we do not renounce escapes us. In a sense, we cannot possess whatever it is without passing through God...

God was able to create only by hiding himself. Otherwise there would be only himself.

Sanctity must also be hidden even, to a certain degree, to the consciousness. And it must be in the world...

It is necessary not to be *myself*; still less to be
  ourselves.
The city makes us feel at home.
We must have the feeling of being at home in exile.
We must be rooted in the absence of a place.

GRAVITY AND GRACE

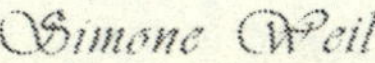

Self-effacement

In all things, only what comes to us from outside freely, unexpectedly, like some sort of unsought after gift, is pure joy...

God's will. How do we know it? If we are silent within ourselves, and quieten all our desires and all our opinions, and if we think lovingly, with all our soul and without words, 'may your will be done', what we then feel without any uncertainty that we must do (even if, in some ways, it may be wrong) is God's will. If we ask him for bread, he does not give us stones...

The real greatness of Christianity lies in that it does not look for a supernatural cure for suffering, but a supernatural use for suffering...

Joy is being fully aware of reality...

We are what is furthest from God, the very outpost from where it is absolutely impossible to come back to him. In us, God is torn apart. We are God's crucifixion. God's love for us is a passion. How could the good not love evil and not suffer? And the evil suffers also in loving the good. The mutual love between God and his creatures is suffering.

GRAVITY AND GRACE

The One we must love is absent

God can only be present in creation under the form of absence...

Nothing that exists is absolutely worthy of love. We must therefore love what does not exist. But this object of love that does not exist is not a fiction. For our fictions can no more be worthy of love than we, who are not, are...

Absolute pure attention is the creative human faculty, and only absolute attention is religious. The number of creative geniuses of a period is directly proportional to the amount of absolute attention and authentic religion of that period.

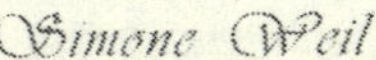

A bad way of searching fixes our attention on a problem. The fear of emptiness is still a phenomenon. We do not want to waste our efforts, relentless in pursuit. We should not want excessively to find the object of our search so that we become dependent on it. We need an exterior reward that sometimes chance brings along and that we are ready to take at the cost of distorting the truth.

GRAVITY AND GRACE

*The Person and the Sacred. Collectivity; person; the
impersonal; rights; justice.*

'I am not interested in you'. No person can say
these words to another without being cruel and
offending against justice...

There is something sacred in every human being.
But it is not the person, nor is it the human
personality. It is, quite simply, this man or this
woman.

I see a passer-by in the street who has long arms,
blue eyes and a mind through which is passing
thoughts of which I am unaware; perhaps, they
are mediocre.

It is neither their person nor the human personality
in them that is sacred to me. The whole person -
the arms, the eyes, the thoughts, everything - I could
not touch any of all that without infinite scruples...

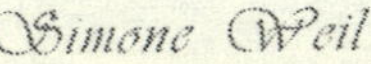
Simone Weil

In the heart of every human being, from earliest childhood to the tomb, there is something, despite every experience of crimes committed, suffered and witnessed, that holds on to the unwavering expectation that good and not evil will be done to them. This, above all, is what is sacred in every human being.

The good is the only source of the sacred. Only the good, and what is related to it is sacred...

That which is sacred and which is quite different from whatever the person in a human being might be, is impersonal.

Everything that is impersonal is sacred, and only that...

Perfection is impersonal. Our personality is that part of us that is wayward and sinful. The mystics put all their efforts into no longer having any part of their soul saying 'I'.

But the part of the soul that says 'we' is infinitely more dangerous still.

We can reach the impersonal only by practising a very rare form of attention which is possible to attain only in solitude - and not just physical solitude but also a moral solitude. It is never reached by a person who thinks of himself or herself as a member of a group, as part of a 'we'...

Beauty is the supreme mystery in this world. It is a brightness that attracts our attention but does not provide a lasting sustenance. Beauty always promises and never gives anything; it stimulates hunger, but it does not have within itself any nourishment for that part of the soul that tries, in this world, to take hold of it. It nourishes only that part of the soul that gazes on it. It arouses desire, but makes it clear that there is nothing in it to desire because, above all, we do not want it to change in any way. If we do not seek ways to get away from the delightful torment it inflicts, desire is gradually transformed into love and a seed of pure and gratuitous attention is formed.

WRITINGS FROM LONDON AND FINAL LETTERS

Simone Weil

Marthe Robin

1902 - 1981

'I no longer know anything,
I no longer know anything but love.'

22 OCTOBER 1936

How can we close this portrait gallery without mentioning the truly atypical figure of Marthe Robin? The person who, without doubt, was 'the strangest, the most extraordinary, the most disconcerting of our times' (Jean Guitton), was perhaps also the most simple.

Born on 13 March 1902, at Châteauneuf-de-Galaure (Drôme), Marthe was the sixth child of a farming family. A delicate child, she showed an ardent desire for prayer from her earliest years. She left school at fourteen to work with her parents

in the fields. In July 1918, she fell seriously ill. She had her first vision of the Blessed Virgin in March 1919. From 1921 on, her health deteriorated yet, despite everything, she kept her sense of humour and her cheerfulness, qualities that never left her. The year 1925 marked a turning point in her life: she consecrated herself to God and she wanted to become a Carmelite like Thérèse of Lisieux who was canonised that year. From then on, Marthe's life was to be a succession of unusual phenomena: in 1930, at the age of twenty-eight, the stigmata appeared; every Friday, until 1981, she suffered the Passion; in October 1927, she had her first 'animal' vision of the devil. From February 1929 on, she became paralysed and was condemned to immobility. Through Père Finet, whom she met on 10 February 1936, this woman, who was infirm and a recluse, was to shine throughout her region, France and then the world.

Père Finet soon became her spiritual director and her constant link to the outside world and the

clergy. She entrusted him with the writing of a prophetic work, *Foyers of Love*. In Marthe's mind, it contained the seed of the Church's 'Pentecost of love', and corresponded to the need for a 'consecrated laity'.

Marthe made her first retreat at Châteauneuf-de-Galaure in 1936. Since then, more than sixty 'Foyers of Charity' have come into being around the world. She died on 6 February 1981, after a life of continual self-offering. Her life had been prey to evil and many undermining factors.

From the age of twenty-five, Marthe dictated her thoughts to people who helped her. The genius of this extraordinary woman was to bring together the following diverse elements in the Church in dynamic fidelity: far-reaching upheavals of renewal, peasant simplicity, 'being cloistered', closeness to individuals and an intuition as quick and accurate as an arrow, by which she was able to see the essence hidden beneath the form. Marthe Robin's mysticism lay in being one with Jesus.

Marthe Robin

The following extracts are translated from *Marthe Robin, la stigmatisée de la Drôme*, by Gonzague Mottet (Érès, 1989) and *Portrait de Marthe Robin* by Jean Guitton (Grasset, 1985).

Act of Abandonment (1926 version)

1. I give and abandon myself to You, Eternal God, Infinite Love! O my Father! You have asked for everything from your little victim; therefore take and receive everything. Today, I give and consecrate myself to You, totally and without reserve.

Beloved of my soul, my sweet Jesus … I want you alone and I renounce everything for the sake of Your love!

My God, take my mind and all my memories; take my heart and all its affections. Take my intellect and all its faculties; use them only for Your greater glory. Take my whole will. I surrender it to Yours forever.

Henceforth, my sweet Jesus, it is no longer what I want, but what you will! Take me… Receive me… Direct me… Guide me!… I give and abandon myself to You!… I give myself to You as a little host of love, of praise and of thanksgiving, for the glory of your

holy Name, to please Your soul, for the triumph of your Sacred Heart and for the perfect fulfilment of all your plans in me and in those around me.

4. I offer myself up for the whole world, O adorable Saviour! You alone possess my soul and my whole being! Receive the offering that, each day and at every moment, I offer You in silence. Deign to accept my offering and to use it for the spiritual and divine good of so many millions of hearts that do not love You, for the conversion of sinners, for the return of the wanderers and the infidels, for the sanctification and apostolate of all Your beloved priests and for all creatures.

6. If I should recoil from suffering … my God, you know my weakness and the immeasurable depths of my misery … If one day I should be unfaithful to your sovereign will for me, if I should recoil from suffering and the Cross and desert your way that is so sweet by fleeing the tender support of your arm, I beg and implore You to give me the grace to die in that moment.

Hear my prayer, O most loving Heart of my God…
Hear my prayer through your most sweet Name of
Jesus, through the intercession of St Joseph, of St
John the Beloved and of all the other saints, and
through your divine Ardour fulfil Your Father's
will in all things.

O my Jesus, Divine Sun of Love! O my Way, my
Light and my Life! I love You, I adore You, I bless
You, I abandon myself to You, I entrust myself to
You. Keep me always wholly Yours; hide me
always completely in You - because my poor nature
trembles and groans beneath the cruel burden of
trials that come upon me from all sides … And I
am always alone.

Marthe Robin

S ince I am the object of the divine good
pleasure, and have no desires, I have no
regrets.

Everything comes to me from God, I am happy
with everything.

I go to Him for everything, with a confident
soul,

for I can always count on his heart.

I have enough to worry me.

It is no longer important for me to know you
well.

The past and the future no longer count for me.

In the present moment, love alone is my law.

I can never have any doubts with Him.

Wonderful Precursor, he straightens my path.

No, I no longer know anything; I no longer
know anything but to love.

I need love more than I need air to breathe.

I feel my heart always beating in my breast,
but I long for divine union.

THE DICTATIONS. 22 OCTOBER 1936

Pentecost

L ord, send forth your Spirit and all will be created, and You will renew the face of the earth.

Lord, renew your first Pentecost. Grant, Jesus, to all your beloved priests, the grace of discernment of spirits, fill them with your gifts, increase their love, make them all valiant apostles and true saints among men.

Holy Spirit, God of Love, come as a powerful wind, into our cathedrals, our churches, our chapels, our cenacles, into the most luxurious houses and the lowliest homes. Fill the whole earth with your lights, your consolations and your love.

Marthe Robin

Come, Spirit of Love, *bring to the world the freshness of your sanctifying breath*. Envelop us all in the light of your grace! Bring all into the splendour of your glory.

Come and comfort today those who are still so burdened with anguish, and brighten the future that is uncertain for many, strengthen those who are still hesitant to walk the divine ways.

Spirit of Light, dispel the darkness of the earth, guide all the wandering sheep to the divine fold, pierce the clouds with your mysterious lights. *Reveal yourself to all and may this day mark the beginning of a new dawn*. Fill all hearts with your many and precious gifts, divine fruit of your sacrifice on Calvary and wondrous token of Christ's promises. Divine Spirit, fire of Love, joy surpassing all riches and light that dispels the most appalling darkness, inspirer of all praise, Spirit of Truth, give all souls the taste for holy things. Bring them into the profound beauty of your mysterious dwelling places. May they enter the secret kingdom

of the divine mysteries as promised by the Word; and their lives wholly transformed, wholly transfigured, wholly divinised in Christ will have infinite power by the very value of your divine riches.

Divine consoler of our sufferings, precious charm of fruitful solitude, cause of all our joy, sacred seed of all spiritual life, spread your immensity throughout the whole universe, *fill the world with your plenitude*. Absorb our human substance into the mystery of your divine unity; imprint in our hearts the seal of the Father's promises; take away the shadow from our faces; let all lips taste the intoxication that comes from Jesus' chalice, and soon a whole harvest of saints will arise in the light.

THE DICTATIONS. 26 MAY 1939

Marthe Robin

Even if I read all the books about the greatest, the most exalted favours God can bestow on a soul, I will still say nothing. This is what happened when I asked to be allowed to read some books to help me explain all I wanted to say about the extraordinary graces I received (which I was refused each time). The Lord chided me severely for this with these words: *in what have I failed you?* Oh! my Jesus, I exclaimed, full of confusion, you have given me everything in abundance, for you have given yourself to me and in you are all perfections and infinite treasures of your grace and gifts. I have drunk freely of the living waters and eaten the good fruit of knowledge. Our Lord, knowing my great poverty and misery, has compassion on my weakness and teaches me himself what He wants me to know and acknowledge. So when someone reads to me out loud, more often than not I do not know what he or

she reads, and I keep only the tiredness that I get from it. *Jesus is for me the book of books* in which he allows me to read constantly and without becoming exhausted. Through this book, the Lord has taught me everything I know and must say and, from the holy tabernacle where He speaks to me, He nourishes me when I am hungry for things so good and so beautiful that they are beyond describing.

But then, I am so stupid that even if I had been able to read, it would be of little benefit to me. I have always felt Our Lord did not want me to read; otherwise, He would have given me the means.

There was a time when I thought that reading the works of some great saints would help me explain more easily what the Lord was doing in me and help me to answer people's questions, but the Lord showed me that such was not his will.

THE DICTATIONS

Marthe Robin